Mix & Match Baby Sampler

It's so easy to bring a fun mix of colors and textures into baby's life! Melissa Leapman presents 12 exciting blocks that you can combine or single out to crochet wonderful wraps. The five afghans featured inside are just a sampling of the endless possibilities.

Sampler 1
Checkerboard.................................. 4
Patchwork 6
Cuddle-Up Baby 8
Naptime 12
Stitch Gallery.................................14
General Instructions.......................28
Yarn Information 31
Meet the Designer..........................32

LEISURE ARTS, INC. • Maumelle, Arkansas

1st Afghan Sampler

●●○○ Easy+

Finished Size: 41" x 54" (104 cm x 137 cm)

Shopping List

Yarn (Medium Weight) [MEDIUM 4]

[5 ounces, 256 yards

(141 grams, 234 meters) per skein]:

- ☐ Jade (B) - 2 skeins
- ☐ Blue (D) - 2 skeins
- ☐ White (F) - 2 skeins
- ☐ Aqua (G) - 2 skeins
- ☐ Yellow (A) - 1 skein
- ☐ Bright Green (C) - 1 skein
- ☐ Purple (E) - 1 skein

Crochet Hook

- ☐ Size I (5.5 mm)

  or size needed for gauge

Additional Supplies

- ☐ Yarn needle

Note: The colors used for this afghan are the ones used in the Stitch Gallery Color Key, page 14.

Gauge Information

Each Square = 6½" (16.5 cm)

Squares

Make a total of 48 squares as follows, pages 16-27:

Make 6 **each** of Squares #5 and #9.

Make 4 **each** of Squares #1, #3, #4, #6, #7, #10, #11, and #12.

Make 2 **each** of Squares #2 and #8.

Block each Square to measure 6½" (16.5 cm) *(see Blocking, page 30)*.

Assembly

With **wrong** sides together and using Placement Diagram as a guide, whipstitch Squares together with White *(Figs. 6a & b, page 30)*, forming 6 vertical strips of 8 Squares each, beginning and ending in corners; then whipstitch strips together in same manner.

Placement Diagram

2	3	6	1	5	7
9	5	8	10	11	4
11	1	12	3	6	12
10	7	9	9	4	5
5	4	9	9	7	10
12	6	3	12	1	11
4	11	10	8	5	9
7	5	1	6	3	2

Edging

Rnd 1: With **right** side of short edge facing, join White with slip st in first corner; ch 1, 3 sc in same corner, ★ † work 22 sc evenly spaced across first Square, work 21 sc evenly spaced across each Square to next corner †, 3 sc in corner; repeat from ★ 2 times **more**, then repeat from † to † once; join with slip st to first sc: 604 sc.

Rnd 2: Ch 1, sc in same st as joining, 3 sc in next corner sc, ★ sc in each sc across to center sc of next corner 3-sc group, 3 sc in corner sc; repeat from ★ 2 times **more**, sc in each sc across; join with slip st to first sc: 612 sc.

Rnd 3: Slip st in next 2 sc, skip next 2 sc, dc in next sc, (ch 1, dc in same st) twice, ★ [skip next 5 sc, dc in next sc, (ch 1, dc in same st) twice] across to within 2 sc of next corner sc, skip next 2 sc, slip st in corner sc, skip next 2 sc, dc in next sc, (ch 1, dc in same st) twice; repeat from ★ 2 times **more**, [skip next 5 sc, dc in next sc, (ch 1, dc in same st) twice] across to last 2 sts, skip last 2 sts; join with slip st to corner slip st, finish off.

2nd Afghan Checkerboard

●●○○ Easy+

Finished Size: 40" (101.5 cm) square

Shopping List

Yarn (Medium Weight) MEDIUM 4

[5 ounces, 256 yards

(141 grams, 234 meters) per skein]:

- ☐ 8 skeins

Crochet Hook

- ☐ Size I (5.5 mm)

  or size needed for gauge

Additional Supplies

- ☐ Yarn needle

Note: The color used for this afghan is the one used in the Stitch Gallery Color Key, page 14.

Gauge Information

Each Square = 6½" (16.5 cm)

Squares

Make 36 Squares of Square #7, page 22.

Block each Square to measure 6½" (16.5 cm) *(see Blocking, page 30)*.

Assembly

With **wrong** sides together, using Placement Diagram as a guide and alternating the direction of each square as shown, whipstitch Squares together *(Figs. 6a & b, page 30)*, forming 6 vertical strips of 6 Squares each, beginning and ending in corners; then whipstitch strips together in same manner.

Placement Diagram

Edging

Rnd 1: With **right** side facing, join yarn with slip st in any corner; ch 1, sc evenly around entire Afghan working 3 sc in each corner; join with slip st to first sc.

Rnd 2: Ch 1, sc in each sc around working 3 sc in each corner sc; join with slip st to first sc.

Rnd 3: Ch 1; working from **left** to **right**, work reverse sc in each sc around *(Figs. 7a-d, page 30)*; join with slip st to first st, finish off.

3rd Afghan Patchwork

●●○○ Easy

Finished Size: 44" x 57" (112 cm x 145 cm)

Shopping List

Yarn (Medium Weight) MEDIUM 4

[5 ounces, 256 yards
(141 grams, 234 meters) per skein]:

- ☐ Blue - 6 skeins
- ☐ Jade - 2 skeins
- ☐ White - 2 skeins
- ☐ Aqua - 1 skein
- ☐ Purple - 1 skein

Crochet Hook

- ☐ Size I (5.5 mm)
  or size needed for gauge

Additional Supplies

- ☐ Yarn needle

Gauge Information

Each Square = 6½" (16.5 cm)

Squares

Make a total of 48 Squares of Square #3, page 18, as follows:

Make 16 Squares using White for Color F and Blue for Color D.

Make 16 Squares using Jade for Color F and Blue for Color D.

Make 8 Squares using Aqua for Color F and Blue for Color D.

Make 8 Squares using Purple for Color F and Blue for Color D.

Block each Square to measure 6½" (16.5 cm) ***(see Blocking, page 30)***.

Instructions continued on page 11.

4th Afghan
Cuddle-Up Baby

●●○○ Easy

Finished Size: 34½" x 47½" (87.5 cm x 120.5 cm)

Shopping List

Yarn (Medium Weight) MEDIUM 4

[5 ounces, 256 yards

(141 grams, 234 meters) per skein]:

- ☐ Yellow - 3 skeins
- ☐ Jade - 2 skeins
- ☐ White - 2 skeins
- ☐ Aqua - 1 skein

Crochet Hook

- ☐ Size I (5.5 mm)

  or size needed for gauge

Additional Supplies

- ☐ Yarn needle

Gauge Information

Each Square = 6½" (16.5 cm)

Squares

Make a total of 35 Squares as follows:

Make 18 of Square #9, page 24.

Make 17 of Square #2, pages 17 and 18, using Jade for Color E.

Block each Square to measure 6½" (16.5 cm) *(see Blocking, page 30)*.

Instructions continued on page 10.

Continued from page 8.

Assembly

With **wrong** sides together and using Placement Diagram as a guide, whipstitch Squares together with Yellow *(Figs. 6a & b, page 30)*, forming 5 vertical strips of 7 Squares each, beginning and ending in corners; then whipstitch strips together in same manner.

Placement Diagram

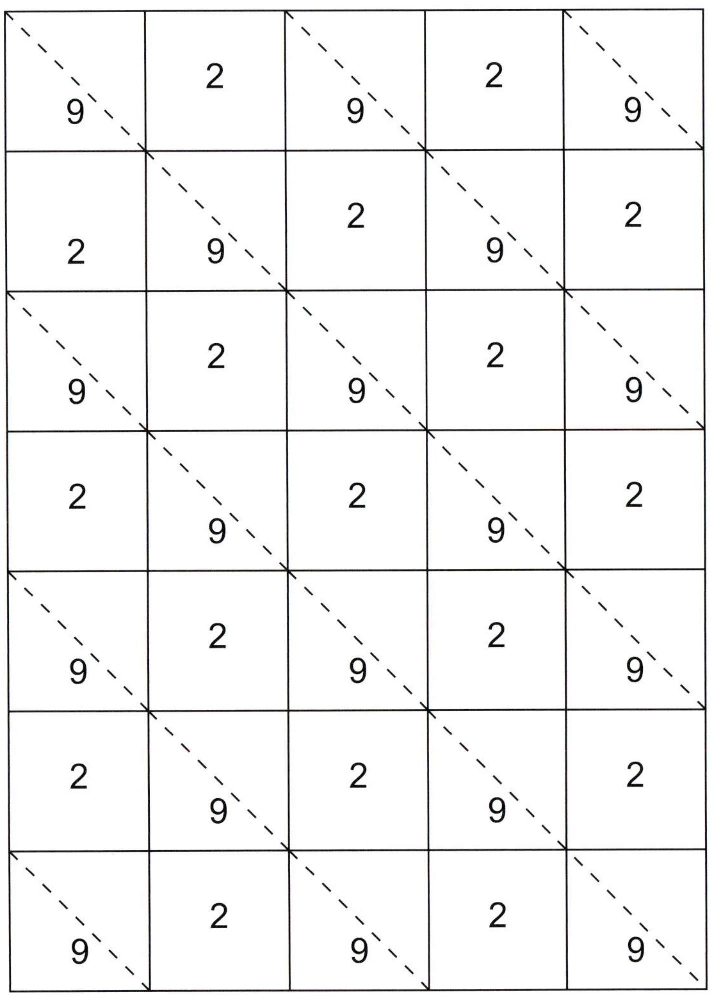

Edging

Rnd 1: With **right** side facing, join Yellow with slip st in any corner; ch 1, 3 sc in same corner, ★ † work 21 sc evenly spaced across each Square to next corner †, 3 sc in corner; repeat from ★ 2 times **more**, then repeat from † to † once; join with slip st to first sc: 516 sc.

Rnd 2: Slip st in next corner sc, ch 4 **(counts as first dc plus ch 1)**, (dc in same st, ch 1) twice, ★ skip next sc, (dc in next sc, ch 1, skip next sc) across to center sc of next corner 3-sc group, (dc, ch 1) 3 times in corner sc; repeat from ★ 2 times **more**, skip next sc, (dc in next sc, ch 1, skip next sc) across; join with slip st to first dc: 266 ch-1 sps.

Rnd 3: (Slip st, ch 1, sc) in next ch-1 sp, ch 3, slip st in third ch from hook, sc in same sp as last sc, ★ sc in next ch-1 sp, ch 3, slip st in third ch from hook, sc in same sp as last sc; repeat from ★ around; join with slip st to first sc, finish off.

Continued from page 6.

Assembly

With **wrong** sides together and using Placement Diagram as a guide, whipstitch Squares together with Blue *(Fig. 6a, page 30)*, forming 6 vertical strips of 8 Squares each, beginning and ending in corner sc; then whipstitch strips together in same manner.

Placement Diagram

Edging

Rnd 1: With **right** side of short edge facing, join Blue with slip st in first corner; ch 1, 3 sc in same corner, † work 23 sc evenly spaced across each Square to next corner, 3 sc in corner, work 22 sc evenly spaced across first Square, work 23 sc evenly spaced across each Square to next corner †, 3 sc in corner; repeat from † to † once; join with slip st to first sc: 654 sc.

Rnd 2: Slip st in next corner sc, ch 5 **(counts as first dc plus ch 2)**, dc in same st, skip next 2 sc, ★ (dc, ch 2, dc) in next sc, skip next 2 sc; repeat from ★ around; join with slip st to first dc: 218 ch-2 sps.

Rnd 3: (Slip st, ch 3, dc, ch 2, 2 dc) in next ch-2 sp, (2 dc, ch 2, 2 dc) in next ch-2 sp and in each ch-2 sp around; join with slip st to first dc.

Rnd 4: Slip st in next dc, (slip st, ch 3, 2 dc) in next ch-2 sp, ch 4, slip st in third ch from hook, ch 1, 3 dc in same sp as last dc, ★ 3 dc in next ch-2 sp, ch 4, slip st in third ch from hook, ch 1, 3 dc in same sp as last dc; repeat from ★ around; join with slip st to first dc, finish off.

5th Afghan
Naptime ●●○○ Easy

Finished Size: 34½" x 47½" (87.5 cm x 120.5 cm)

Shopping List

Yarn (Medium Weight) MEDIUM 4
[5 ounces, 256 yards
(141 grams, 234 meters) per skein]:

- ☐ Bright Green (C) - 4 skeins
- ☐ Yellow (A) - 2 skeins
- ☐ Jade (B) - 2 skeins

Crochet Hook

- ☐ Size I (5.5 mm)
  or size needed for gauge

Additional Supplies

- ☐ Yarn needle

Note: The colors used for this afghan are the ones used in the Stitch Gallery Color Key, page 14.

Gauge Information

Each Square = 6½" (16.5 cm)

Squares

Make 35 Squares of Square #4, page 19.

Block each Square to measure 6½" (16.5 cm) *(see Blocking, page 30)*.

Assembly

With **wrong** sides together, whipstitch Squares together with Bright Green *(Fig. 6a, page 30)*, forming 5 vertical strips of 7 Squares each, beginning and ending in corner chs; then whipstitch strips together in the same manner.

Edging

Rnd 1: With **right** side of short edge facing, join Bright Green with slip st in first corner; ch 1, 3 sc in same corner, ★ † work 22 sc evenly spaced across first 2 Squares, work 23 sc evenly spaced across each Square to next corner †, 3 sc in corner; repeat from ★ 2 times **more**, then repeat from † to † once; join with slip st to first sc: 556 sc.

Rnd 2: Slip st in next corner sc, ch 4 **(counts as first dc plus ch 1)**, (dc in same st, ch 1) twice, ★ skip next sc, (dc in next sc, ch 1, skip next sc) across to center sc of next corner 3-sc group, (dc, ch 1) 3 times in corner sc; repeat from ★ 2 times **more**, skip next sc, (dc in next sc, ch 1, skip next sc) across; join with slip st to first dc: 286 ch-1 sps.

Rnd 3: Slip st in next ch-1 sp, (sc, 2 dc, sc) in same sp and in each ch-1 sp around; join with slip st to first sc, finish off.

HarperCollins

Stitch Gallery

Finished Size: 6½" (16.5 cm) square

We used Medium Weight Yarn and a size I (5.5 mm) crochet hook for all the photographed Squares. **Use the size hook needed to achieve a 6½" (16.5 cm) square.**

Color Key

Color A (Yellow)	Color E (Purple)
Color B (Jade)	Color F (White)
Color C (Bright Green)	Color G (Aqua)
Color D (Blue)	

#1

#2

#3

#4

#5

#6

#7

#8

#9

#10

#11

#12

Instructions for all Squares are on pages 16-27.

#1 Easy+

Yarn Requirements for one square:

Color C - 26 yards (24 meters)
Color D - 17 yards (15.5 meters)

Rnd 1 (Right side)**:** With Color C, ch 2, 6 sc in second ch from hook; join with slip st to first sc, finish off.

Note: Loop a short piece of yarn around any stitch to mark Rnd 1 as **right** side.

Rnd 2: With **right** side facing, join Color D with slip st in any sc; ch 1, 2 sc in same st and in each sc around; join with slip st to first sc: 12 sc.

Rnd 3: Ch 1, 2 sc in same st as joining, sc in next sc, (2 sc in next sc, sc in next sc) around; join with slip st to first sc: 18 sc.

Rnd 4: Ch 1, sc in same st as joining, ch 1, sc in next sc, 3 dc in next sc, ★ sc in next sc, ch 1, sc in next sc, 3 dc in next sc; repeat from ★ around; join with slip st to first sc, finish off: 30 sts and 6 ch-1 sps.

To work Front Post Treble Crochet *(abbreviated FPtr)*, YO twice, insert hook from **front** to **back** around post of st indicated *(Fig. 3, page 29)*, YO and pull up a loop (4 loops on hook), (YO and draw through 2 loops on hook) 3 times.

Rnd 5: With **right** side facing and working in Front Loops Only *(Fig. 1, page 28)*, join Color C with slip st in center dc of any 3-dc group; ch 1, 3 sc in same st, ch 1, skip next 2 sts, work FPtr around sc 3 rnds **below** next ch (on Rnd 1), ch 1, skip next 2 sts, ★ 3 sc in next dc, ch 1, skip next 2 sts, work FPtr around sc 3 rnds **below** next ch, ch 1, skip next 2 sts; repeat from ★ around; join with slip st to **both** loops of first sc, finish off: 24 sts and 12 ch-1 sps.

Rnd 6: With **right** side facing and working in free loops of sts *(Fig. 2, page 29)* and in Back Loops Only on Rnd 4 *(Fig. 1, page 28)*, join Color D with slip st in center dc of any 3-dc group; ch 1, sc in same st and in next dc, skip next sc, 3 dc in next ch-1 sp, ★ skip next sc, sc in next 3 dc, skip next sc, 3 dc in next ch-1 sp; repeat from ★ around to last 2 sts, skip next sc, sc in last dc; join with slip st to **both** loops of first sc: 36 sts.

Rnd 7: Ch 1, working in both loops, sc in same st as joining and in next 2 sts, 2 sc in next dc, (sc in next 5 sts, 2 sc in next dc) around to last 2 sts, sc in last 2 sts; join with slip st to first sc: 42 sc.

Rnd 8: Ch 1, sc in same st as joining and in next 3 sc, 2 sc in next sc, (sc in next 6 sc, 2 sc in next sc) around to last 2 sc, sc in last 2 sc; join with slip st to first sc, finish off: 48 sc.

To work treble crochet *(abbreviated tr)*, YO twice, insert hook in st indicated, YO and pull up a loop (4 loops on hook), (YO and draw through 2 loops on hook) 3 times.

Rnd 9: With **right** side facing, join Color C with slip st in same st as joining; ch 1, sc in same st, working in **front** of previous 3 rnds *(Fig. 5, page 30)*, tr in center sc of next 3-sc group on Rnd 5, sc in next 4 sc on Rnd 8, working in **front** of previous 3 rnds, tr in same sc as last tr made, ★ sc in next 4 sc on Rnd 8, working in **front** of previous 3 rnds, tr in center sc of next 3-sc group on Rnd 5, sc in next 4 sc on Rnd 8, working in **front** of previous 3 rnds, tr in same sc as last tr made; repeat from ★ around to last 3 sc, sc in last 3 sc; join with slip st to first sc: 60 sts.

Rnd 10: Ch 1, sc in same st as joining, ch 4, skip next 4 sts, (dc, ch 3, dc) in next sc (corner made), ch 4, ★ skip next 4 sts, (sc in next sc, ch 4, skip next 4 sts) twice, (dc, ch 3, dc) in next sc (corner made), ch 4; repeat from ★ 2 times **more**, skip next 4 sts, sc in next sc, ch 4, skip last 4 sts; join with slip st to first sc: 16 sts and 16 sps.

Rnd 11: Ch 1, sc in same st as joining, 4 sc in next ch-4 sp, sc in next dc, (2 sc, ch 2, 2 sc) in next ch-3 sp, sc in next dc, ★ 4 sc in next ch-4 sp, (sc in next sc, 4 sc in next ch-4 sp) twice, sc in next dc, (2 sc, ch 2, 2 sc) in next ch-3 sp, sc in next dc; repeat from ★ 2 times **more**, 4 sc in next ch-4 sp, sc in next sc, 4 sc in last ch-4 sp; join with slip st to first sc: 80 sc and 4 corner ch-2 sps.

Rnd 12: Ch 1, sc in same st as joining and in next 7 sc, 3 sc in next corner ch-2 sp, (sc in next 20 sc, 3 sc in next corner ch-2 sp) 3 times, sc in last 12 sc; join with slip st to first sc, finish off: 92 sc. ✤

#2 ●●○○ Easy

Yarn Requirements for one square:
Color A - 16 yards (14.5 meters)
Color E - 21 yards (19 meters)

With Color E, ch 4; join with slip st to form a ring.

Rnd 1 (Right side)**:** Ch 3 **(counts as first dc, now and throughout)**, 2 dc in ring, ch 3, (3 dc in ring, ch 3) 3 times; join with slip st to first dc changing to Color A *(Fig. A)*, do **not** cut Color E: 12 dc and 4 ch-3 sps.

Fig. A

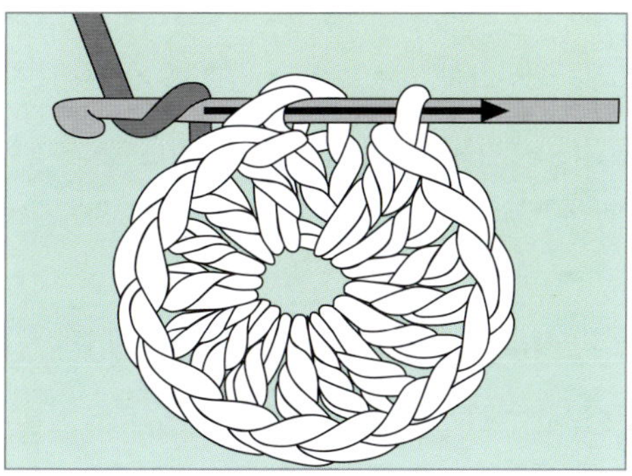

Note: Loop a short piece of yarn around any stitch to mark Rnd 1 as **right** side.

Change colors in same manner throughout; do **not** cut yarn until instructed.

Rnd 2: Ch 1, sc in same st as joining and in next 2 dc, working **around** next ch-3 *(Fig. 5, page 30)*, (dc, ch 3, dc) in beginning ring (between 3-dc groups), ★ sc in next 3 dc, working **around** next ch-3, (dc, ch 3, dc) in beginning ring (between 3-dc groups); repeat from ★ 2 times **more**; join with slip st to first sc changing to Color E: 20 sts and 4 ch-3 sps.

Rnd 3: Ch 3, dc in next 3 sts, (dc, ch 3, dc) in next ch-3 sp, ★ dc in next 5 sts, (dc, ch 3, dc) in next ch-3 sp; repeat from ★ 2 times **more**, dc in last dc; join with slip st to first dc changing to Color A: 28 dc and 4 ch-3 sps.

Rnd 4: Ch 1, sc in same st as joining and in next 4 dc, working **around** next ch-3, (dc, ch 3, dc) in ch-3 sp on Rnd 2, ★ sc in next 7 dc, working **around** next ch-3, (dc, ch 3, dc) in ch-3 sp on Rnd 2; repeat from ★ 2 times **more**, sc in last 2 dc; join with slip st to first sc changing to Color E: 36 sts and 4 ch-3 sps.

Rnd 5: Ch 3, dc in next 5 sts, (dc, ch 3, dc) in next ch-3 sp, ★ dc in next 9 sts, (dc, ch 3, dc) in next ch-3 sp; repeat from ★ 2 times **more**, dc in last 3 sts; join with slip st to first dc changing to Color A: 44 dc and 4 ch-3 sps.

Rnd 6: Ch 1, sc in same st as joining and in next 6 dc, working **around** next ch-3, (dc, ch 3, dc) in ch-3 sp on Rnd 4, ★ sc in next 11 dc, working **around** next ch-3, (dc, ch 3, dc) in ch-3 sp on Rnd 4; repeat from ★ 2 times **more**, sc in last 4 dc; join with slip st to first sc changing to Color E: 52 sts and 4 ch-3 sps.

Rnd 7: Ch 3, dc in next 7 sts, (dc, ch 3, dc) in next ch-3 sp, ★ dc in next 13 sts, (dc, ch 3, dc) in next ch-3 sp; repeat from ★ 2 times **more**, dc in last 5 sts; join with slip st to first dc changing to Color A; cut Color E: 60 dc and 4 ch-3 sps.

Rnd 8: Ch 1, sc in same st as joining and in next 8 dc, working **around** next ch-3, (dc, ch 3, dc) in ch-3 sp on Rnd 6, ★ sc in next 15 dc, working **around** next ch-3, (dc, ch 3, dc) in ch-3 sp on Rnd 6; repeat from ★ 2 times **more**, sc in last 6 dc; join with slip st to first sc, finish off: 68 sts and 4 ch-3 sps. ✤

#3 ●●○○ Easy

Yarn Requirements for one square:

Color D - 26 yards (24 meters)

Color F - 18 yards (16.5 meters)

With Color F, ch 4; join with slip st to form a ring.

Rnd 1 (Right side)**:** Ch 3 **(counts as first dc, now and throughout)**, 15 dc in ring; join with slip st to first dc: 16 dc.

Note: Loop a short piece of yarn around any stitch to mark Rnd 1 as **right** side.

To work beginning Cluster (uses one st or sp), ch 3, dc in st or sp indicated.

To work Cluster (uses one st or sp), ★ YO, insert hook in st or sp indicated, YO and pull up a loop, YO and draw through 2 loops on hook; repeat from ★ once **more**, YO and draw through all 3 loops on hook.

Rnd 2: Work (beginning Cluster, ch 2, Cluster) in same st as joining, ch 2, skip next dc, ★ (work Cluster, ch 2) twice in next dc, skip next dc; repeat from ★ around; join with slip st to top of beginning Cluster: 16 Clusters and 16 ch-2 sps.

Rnd 3: Slip st in next ch-2 sp, work (beginning Cluster, ch 2, Cluster) in same sp, ch 2, sc in next ch-2 sp, ch 2, ★ (work Cluster, ch 2) twice in next ch-2 sp, sc in next ch-2 sp, ch 2; repeat from ★ around; join with slip st to top of beginning Cluster: 16 Clusters and 24 ch-2 sps.

Rnd 4: Slip st in next ch-2 sp, work (beginning Cluster, ch 2, Cluster) in same sp, ch 7, skip next 2 ch-2 sps, ★ work (Cluster, ch 2, Cluster) in next ch-2 sp, ch 7, skip next 2 ch-2 sps; repeat from ★ around; join with slip st to top of beginning Cluster, finish off: 16 Clusters and 16 sps.

Rnd 5: With **right** side facing, join Color D with slip st in any ch-2 sp; ch 3, (2 dc, ch 3, 3 dc) in same sp, ch 4, working **around** previous 2 rnds *(Fig. 5, page 30)*, sc in next ch-2 sp 3 rnds **below** (on Rnd 2), ch 4, sc in next ch-2 sp, ch 4, working **around** previous 2 rnds, sc in next ch-2 sp 3 rnds **below**, ch 4, ★ (3 dc, ch 3, 3 dc) in next ch-2 sp, ch 4, working **around** previous 2 rnds, sc in next ch-2 sp 3 rnds **below**, ch 4, sc in next ch-2 sp, ch 4, working **around**

previous 2 rnds, sc in next ch-2 sp 3 rnds **below**, ch 4; repeat from ★ 2 times **more**; join with slip st to first dc: 36 sts and 20 sps.

Rnd 6: Slip st in next 2 dc and in next ch-3 sp, ch 1, (sc, ch 3, sc) in same sp, ch 4, working **around** previous 3 rnds, dc in same ch-2 sp 4 rnds **below**, ch 4, slip st in next sc, ch 4, working **around** previous 3 rnds, dc in same ch-2 sp 4 rnds **below**, ch 4, ★ (sc, ch 3, sc) in next ch-3 sp, ch 4, working **around** previous 3 rnds, dc in same ch-2 sp 4 rnds **below**, ch 4, slip st in next sc, ch 4, working **around** previous 3 rnds, dc in same ch-2 sp 4 rnds **below**, ch 4; repeat from ★ 2 times **more**; join with slip st to first sc.

Rnd 7: (Slip st, ch 1, 5 sc) in next ch-3 sp, 4 sc in each of next 4 ch-4 sps, ★ 5 sc in next ch-3 sp, 4 sc in each of next 4 ch-4 sps; repeat from ★ 2 times **more**; join with slip st to first sc: 84 sc.

Rnd 8: Ch 1, sc in same st as joining and in next sc, 3 sc in next corner sc, (sc in next 20 sc, 3 sc in next corner sc) 3 times, sc in last 18 sc; join with slip st to first sc, finish off: 92 sc. ✤

#4

●●○○ Easy

Yarn Requirements for one square:

Color A - 11 yards (10 meters)
Color B - 11 yards (10 meters)
Color C - 19 yards (17.5 meters)

With Color A, ch 5; join with slip st to form a ring.

Rnd 1 (Right side)**:** Ch 3 **(counts as first dc, now and throughout)**, 23 dc in ring; join with slip st to first dc: 24 dc.

Note: Loop a short piece of yarn around any stitch to mark Rnd 1 as **right** side.

Rnd 2: Ch 6, sc in second ch from hook, dc in next 4 chs, skip same st as joining and next 2 dc, ★ slip st in next dc, ch 6, sc in second ch from hook, dc in next 4 chs, skip next 2 dc; repeat from ★ around; join with slip st to dc at base of beginning ch-6, finish off: 8 spokes.

To work double treble crochet *(abbreviated dtr)*, YO 3 times, insert hook in st indicated, YO and pull up a loop (5 loops on hook), (YO and draw through 2 loops on hook) 4 times.

Rnd 3: With **right** side facing, join Color B with slip st in tip of any spoke; ch 1, sc in same st, working **around** next slip st *(Fig. 5, page 30)*, 4 dtr in same dc on Rnd 1 as slip st, ★ sc in tip of next spoke, working **around** next slip st, 4 dtr in same dc on Rnd 1 as slip st; repeat from ★ around; join with slip st to first sc, finish off: 32 dtr and 8 sc.

Rnd 4: With **right** side facing, join Color C with slip st in same sc as joining; ch 3, (2 dc, ch 3, 3 dc) in same st, ch 5, skip next 4 dtr, sc in next sc, ch 5, skip next 4 dtr, ★ (3 dc, ch 3, 3 dc) in next sc, ch 5, skip next 4 dtr, sc in next sc, ch 5, skip next 4 dtr; repeat from ★ 2 times **more**; join with slip st to first dc: 28 sts and 12 sps.

Rnd 5: Ch 3, dc in next 2 dc, (2 dc, ch 3, 2 dc) in next ch-3 sp, ★ † dc in next 3 dc, 5 dc in next ch-5 sp, dc in next sc, 5 dc in next ch-5 sp †, dc in next 3 dc, (2 dc, ch 3, 2 dc) in next ch-3 sp; repeat from ★ 2 times **more**, then repeat from † to † once; join with slip st to first dc, finish off: 84 dc and 4 ch-3 sps. ✤

#5

●●○○ Easy

Yarn Requirements for one square:
Color G - 43 yards (39.5 meters)

Ch 4; join with slip st to form a ring.

Rnd 1 (Right side)**:** Ch 1, 8 sc in ring; join with slip st to first sc.

Note: Loop a short piece of yarn around any stitch to mark Rnd 1 as **right** side.

Rnd 2: Ch 1, 2 sc in same st as joining and in each sc around; join with slip st to first sc: 16 sc.

Rnd 3: Ch 8 **(counts as first dc plus ch 5)**, dc in sixth ch from hook, skip next sc, ★ dc in next sc, ch 5, dc in top of last dc made, skip next sc; repeat from ★ around; join with slip st to first dc: 16 dc and 8 ch-5 sps.

Rnd 4: Ch 5 **(counts as first dc plus ch 2)**, sc in next ch-5 sp, ch 2, skip next dc, ★ dc in next dc, ch 2, sc in next ch-5 sp, ch 2, skip next dc; repeat from ★ around; join with slip st to first dc: 16 sts and 16 ch-2 sps.

Rnd 5: Ch 3 **(counts as first dc, now and throughout)**, (2 dc, ch 3, 3 dc) in same st as joining, ch 3, skip next 2 ch-2 sps, dc in next dc, ch 3, skip next 2 ch-2 sps, ★ (3 dc, ch 3) twice in next dc, skip next 2 ch-2 sps, dc in next dc, ch 3, skip next 2 ch-2 sps; repeat from ★ 2 times **more**; join with slip st to first dc: 28 dc and 12 ch-3 sps.

Rnd 6: Ch 3, dc in next 2 dc, ★ † (dc, ch 3, dc) in next ch-3 sp (corner made), dc in next 3 dc, 3 dc in next ch-3 sp, dc in next dc, 3 dc in next ch-3 sp †, dc in next 3 dc; repeat from ★ 2 times **more**, then repeat from † to † once; join with slip st to first dc: 60 dc and 4 corner ch-3 sps.

Rnd 7: Ch 3, dc in next 3 dc, (dc, ch 3, dc) in next corner ch-3 sp, ★ dc in next 15 dc, (dc, ch 3, dc) in next corner ch-3 sp; repeat from ★ 2 times **more**, dc in last 11 dc; join with slip st to first dc: 68 dc and 4 corner ch-3 sps.

Rnd 8: Ch 1, sc in same st as joining and in next 4 dc, 5 sc in next corner ch-3 sp, ★ sc in next 17 dc, 5 sc in next corner ch-3 sp; repeat from ★ 2 times **more**, sc in last 12 dc; join with slip st to first sc, finish off: 88 sc. ✤

#6

●●○○ Easy+

Yarn Requirements for one square:

Color D - 17 yards (15.5 meters)
Color E - 7 yards (6.5 meters)
Color F - 8 yards (7.5 meters)
Color G - 12 yards (11 meters)

With Color F, ch 4; join with slip st to form a ring.

Rnd 1 (Right side)**:** Ch 3 **(counts as first dc, now and throughout)**, 2 dc in ring, ch 2, (3 dc in ring, ch 2) 3 times; join with slip st to first dc: 12 dc and 4 ch-2 sps.

Note: Loop a short piece of yarn around any stitch to mark Rnd 1 as **right** side.

Rnd 2: Ch 3, dc in next 2 dc, (dc, ch 9, dc) in next ch-2 sp, working in **front** of second dc made, dc in top of first dc (corner dc made), ★ dc in next 3 dc, (dc, ch 9, dc) in next ch-2 sp, working in **front** of second dc made, dc in top of first dc (corner dc made); repeat from ★ 2 times **more**; join with slip st to first dc changing to Color G *(Fig. A)*, **cut old color, now and throughout**; pull each loop from **back** to **front under** corner dc, making sure they are **not** twisted: 24 dc and 4 loops.

Fig. A

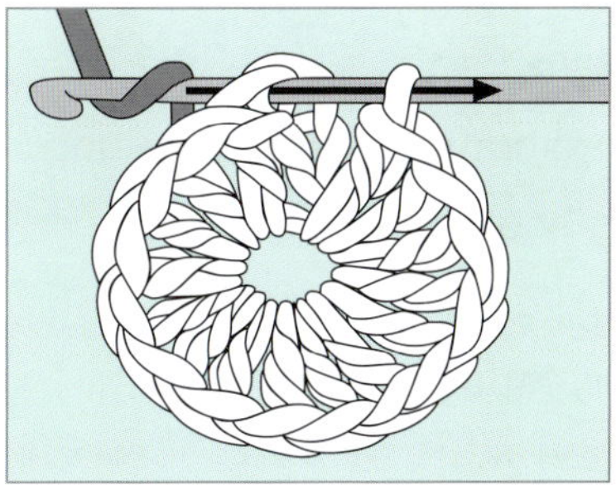

Rnd 3: Ch 3, dc in next 3 dc, ★ † keeping loop to the **front**, (dc, ch 3, dc) **around** corner dc †, dc in top of same corner dc and in next 4 dc; repeat from ★ 2 times **more**, then repeat from † to † once, dc in top of same corner dc; join with slip st to first dc: 28 dc and 4 ch-3 sps.

Rnd 4: Ch 3, dc in next 4 dc and in next ch-3 sp, (dc, ch 9, dc) in next loop on Rnd 2, working in **front** of second dc made, dc in top of first dc (corner dc made), dc in same ch-3 sp on Rnd 3, ★ dc in next 7 dc and in next ch-3 sp, (dc, ch 9, dc) in next loop on Rnd 2, working in **front** of second dc made, dc in top of first dc (corner dc made), dc in same ch-3 sp on Rnd 3; repeat from ★ 2 times **more**, dc in last 2 dc; join with slip st to first dc changing to Color D; pull each loop from **back** to **front under** corner dc, making sure they are **not** twisted: 48 dc and 4 loops.

Rnd 5: Ch 3, dc in next 5 dc, skip next dc, ★ † keeping loop to the **front**, (dc, ch 3, dc) **around** corner dc, skip top of same corner dc †, dc in next 9 dc; repeat from ★ 2 times **more**, then repeat from † to † once, dc in last 3 dc; join with slip st to first dc: 44 dc and 4 ch-3 sps.

Rnd 6: Ch 3, dc in next 6 dc and in next ch-3 sp, (dc, ch 5, dc) in next loop on Rnd 4, working in **front** of second dc made, dc in top of first dc (corner dc made), dc in same ch-3 sp on Rnd 5, ★ dc in next 11 dc and in next ch-3 sp, (dc, ch 5, dc) in next loop on Rnd 4, working in **front** of second dc made, dc in top of first dc (corner dc made), dc in same ch-3 sp on Rnd 5; repeat from ★ 2 times **more**, dc in last 4 dc; join with slip st to first dc changing to Color E; pull each loop from **back** to **front under** corner dc, making sure they are **not** twisted: 64 dc and 4 loops.

Rnd 7: Ch 1, sc in same st as joining and in next 7 dc, 5 sc in next loop on Rnd 6, skip same 2 corner dc, ★ sc in next 13 dc, 5 sc in next loop on Rnd 6, skip same 2 corner dc; repeat from ★ 2 times **more**, sc in last 5 dc; join with slip st to first dc, finish off: 72 sc. ✤

#7 Easy+

Yarn Requirements for one square:
Color D - 50 yards (45.5 meters)

Ch 22.

Row 1: Sc in second ch from hook and in each ch across: 21 sc.

Row 2 (Right side)**:** Ch 2 **(counts as first hdc, now and throughout)**, turn; hdc in next sc and in each sc across.

Note: Loop a short piece of yarn around any stitch to mark Row 2 as **right** side.

Row 3: Ch 2, turn; hdc in next hdc and in each hdc across.

To work Front Post treble crochet *(abbreviated FPtr)*, YO twice, insert hook from **front** to **back** around post of st indicated *(Fig. 3, page 29)*, YO and pull up a loop (4 loops on hook), (YO and draw through 2 loops on hook) 3 times.

To work Popcorn (uses one hdc), 5 dc in hdc indicated, drop loop from hook, insert hook in first dc of 5-dc group, hook dropped loop and draw through dc.

Row 4: Ch 2, turn; hdc in next hdc, work FPtr around each of next 2 hdc 2 rows **below** (on Row 2), skip next 2 hdc from last hdc made, ★ hdc in next hdc, work Popcorn in next hdc, hdc in next hdc, work FPtr around each of next 2 hdc 2 rows **below** (on Row 2), skip next 2 hdc from last hdc made; repeat from ★ across to last 2 hdc, hdc in last 2 hdc: 10 hdc, 8 FPtr, and 3 Popcorns.

Row 5: Ch 2, turn; hdc in next hdc and in each st across: 21 hdc.

Row 6: Ch 2, turn; hdc in next hdc, work FPtr around each of next 2 FPtr 2 rows **below**, skip next 2 hdc from last hdc made, ★ hdc in next 3 hdc, work FPtr around each of next 2 FPtr 2 rows **below**, skip next 2 hdc from last hdc made; repeat from ★ across to last 2 hdc, hdc in last 2 hdc: 13 hdc and 8 FPtr.

Row 7: Ch 2, turn; hdc in next hdc and in each st across: 21 hdc.

Row 8: Ch 2, turn; hdc in next hdc, work FPtr around each of next 2 FPtr 2 rows **below**, skip next 2 hdc from last hdc made, ★ hdc in next hdc, work Popcorn in next hdc, hdc in next hdc, work FPtr around each of next 2 FPtr 2 rows **below**, skip next 2 hdc from last hdc made; repeat from ★ across to last 2 hdc, hdc in last 2 hdc: 10 hdc, 8 FPtr, and 3 Popcorns.

Rows 9-17: Repeat Rows 5-8 twice, then repeat Row 5 once **more**.

Row 18: Ch 1, turn; sc in each hdc across; finish off. ✤

#8

●●○○ Easy

Yarn Requirements for one square:

Color A - 22 yards (20 meters)
Color B - 22 yards (20 meters)

With Color A, ch 5; join with slip st to form a ring.

Rnd 1: Ch 3 **(counts as first dc, now and throughout)**, 2 dc in ring, ch 2, 3 dc in ring, ch 1, drop Color A; with Color B, ch 1, (3 dc in ring, ch 2) twice; join with slip st to first dc: 12 dc and 4 corner ch-2 sps.

Rnd 2 (Right side)**:** Turn; with Color B, (slip st, ch 3, 2 dc) in first corner ch-2 sp, ch 1, (3 dc, ch 2, 3 dc) in next corner ch-2 sp, ch 1, 3 dc in next corner ch-2 sp, ch 1, drop Color B; with Color A, ch 1, 3 dc in same corner sp, ch 1, (3 dc, ch 2, 3 dc) in next corner ch-2 sp, ch 1, 3 dc in same corner sp as first 3 dc, ch 2; join with slip st to first dc: 24 dc and 8 sps.

Note: Loop a short piece of yarn around any stitch to mark Rnd 2 as **right** side.

Rnd 3: Turn; with Color A, (slip st, ch 3, 2 dc) in first corner ch-2 sp, ch 1, 3 dc in next ch-1 sp, ch 1, (3 dc, ch 2, 3 dc) in next corner ch-2 sp, ch 1, 3 dc in next ch-1 sp, ch 1, 3 dc in next corner ch-2 sp, ch 1, drop Color A; with Color B, ch 1, 3 dc in same corner sp, ch 1, 3 dc in next ch-1 sp, ch 1, (3 dc, ch 2, 3 dc) in next corner ch-2 sp, ch 1, 3 dc in next ch-1 sp, ch 1, 3 dc in same corner sp as first 3 dc, ch 2; join with slip st to first dc: 36 dc and 12 sps.

Rnd 4: Turn; with Color B, (slip st, ch 3, 2 dc) in first corner ch-2 sp, ch 1, (3 dc in next ch-1 sp, ch 1) twice, (3 dc, ch 2, 3 dc) in next corner ch-2 sp, ch 1, (3 dc in next ch-1 sp, ch 1) twice, 3 dc in next corner ch-2 sp, ch 1, drop Color B; with Color A, ch 1, 3 dc in same corner sp, ch 1, (3 dc in next ch-1 sp, ch 1) twice, (3 dc, ch 2, 3 dc) in next corner ch-2 sp, ch 1, (3 dc in next ch-1 sp, ch 1) twice, 3 dc in same corner sp as first 3 dc, ch 2; join with slip st to first dc: 48 dc and 16 sps.

Rnd 5: Turn; with Color A, (slip st, ch 3, 2 dc) in first corner ch-2 sp, ch 1, (3 dc in next ch-1 sp, ch 1) 3 times, (3 dc, ch 2, 3 dc) in next corner ch-2 sp, ch 1, (3 dc in next ch-1 sp, ch 1) 3 times, 3 dc in next corner ch-2 sp, ch 1, drop Color A; with Color B, ch 1, 3 dc in same corner sp, ch 1, (3 dc in next ch-1 sp, ch 1) 3 times, (3 dc, ch 2, 3 dc) in next corner ch-2 sp, ch 1, (3 dc in next ch-1 sp, ch 1) 3 times, 3 dc in same corner sp as first 3 dc, ch 2; join with slip st to first dc: 60 dc and 20 sps.

Rnd 6: Turn; with Color B, (slip st, ch 3, 2 dc) in first corner ch-2 sp, ch 1, (3 dc in next ch-1 sp, ch 1) 4 times, (3 dc, ch 2, 3 dc) in next corner ch-2 sp, ch 1, (3 dc in next ch-1 sp, ch 1) 4 times, 3 dc in next corner ch-2 sp, ch 1, cut Color B; with Color A, ch 1, 3 dc in same corner sp, ch 1, (3 dc in next ch-1 sp, ch 1) 4 times, (3 dc, ch 2, 3 dc) in next corner ch-2 sp, ch 1, (3 dc in next ch-1 sp, ch 1) 4 times, 3 dc in same corner sp as first 3 dc, ch 2; join with slip st to first dc, finish off: 72 dc and 24 sps. ✤

#9

●●○○ Easy

Yarn Requirements for one square:

Color A - 12 yards (11 meters)
Color B - 5 yards (4.5 meters)
Color F - 20 yards (18.5 meters)
Color G - 7 yards (6.5 meters)

With Color F, ch 4.

Row 1 (Right side)**:** 3 Dc in fourth ch from hook (**3 skipped chs count as first dc**): 4 dc.

Note: Loop a short piece of yarn around any stitch to mark Row 1 as **right** side.

Row 2: Ch 3 (**counts as first dc, now and throughout**), turn; dc in first dc and in next 2 dc, 2 dc in last dc: 6 dc.

Row 3: Ch 3, turn; 2 dc in first dc, dc in next 4 dc, 3 dc in last dc changing to Color B in last dc *(Fig. 4b, page 29)*, **cut old color, now and throughout**: 10 dc.

Row 4: Ch 3, turn; dc in first dc and in next 8 dc, 2 dc in last dc changing to Color F in last dc: 12 dc.

Row 5: Ch 3, turn; 2 dc in first dc, dc in next 10 dc, 3 dc in last dc: 16 dc.

Row 6: Ch 3, turn; dc in first dc and in next 14 dc, 2 dc in last dc: 18 dc.

Row 7: Ch 3, turn; 2 dc in first dc, dc in next 16 dc, 3 dc in last dc changing to Color G in last dc: 22 dc.

Row 8: Ch 3, turn; dc in first dc and in next 20 dc, 2 dc in last dc changing to Color A in last dc: 24 dc.

Row 9: Ch 3, turn; 2 dc in first dc, dc in next 22 dc, 3 dc in last dc: 28 dc.

Row 10: Ch 3, turn; dc in first dc and in next 26 dc, 2 dc in last dc: 30 dc.

To double crochet 2 together *(abbreviated dc2tog)*, ★ YO, insert hook in **next** dc, YO and pull up a loop, YO and draw through 2 loops on hook; repeat from ★ once **more**, YO and draw through all 3 loops on hook (**counts as one dc**).

Row 11: Ch 3, turn; dc2tog, dc in next 24 dc, dc2tog, dc in last dc changing to Color G: 28 dc.

Row 12: Ch 3, turn; dc2tog twice, dc in next 18 dc, dc2tog twice, dc in last dc changing to Color F: 24 dc.

Row 13: Ch 3, turn; dc2tog, dc in next 18 dc, dc2tog, dc in last dc: 22 dc.

Row 14: Ch 3, turn; dc2tog twice, dc in next 12 dc, dc2tog twice, dc in last dc: 18 dc.

Row 15: Ch 3, turn; dc2tog, dc in next 12 dc, dc2tog, dc in last dc changing to Color B: 16 dc.

Row 16: Ch 3, turn; dc2tog twice, dc in next 6 dc, dc2tog twice, dc in last dc changing to Color F: 12 dc.

Row 17: Ch 3, turn; dc2tog, dc in next 6 dc, dc2tog, dc in last dc: 10 dc.

Row 18: Ch 3, turn; dc2tog 4 times, dc in last dc: 6 dc.

Row 19: Ch 3, turn; dc2tog twice, dc in last dc; finish off: 4 dc. ✤

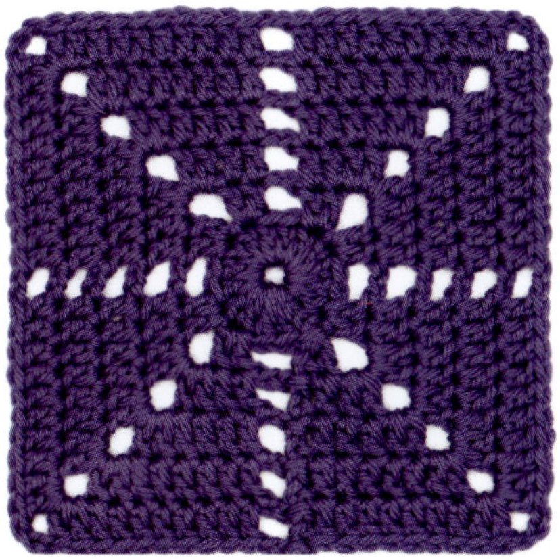

#10 ●●○○ Easy

Yarn Requirements for one square:
Color E - 39 yards (35.5 meters)

Ch 5; join with slip st to form a ring.

Rnd 1 (Right side): Ch 3 **(counts as first dc, now and throughout)**, 15 dc in ring; join with slip st to first dc: 16 dc.

Note: Loop a short piece of yarn around any stitch to mark Rnd 1 as **right** side.

Rnd 2: Ch 3, dc in same st as joining, ch 3, 2 dc in next dc, ch 2, skip next 2 dc, ★ 2 dc in next dc, ch 3, 2 dc in next dc, ch 2, skip next 2 dc; repeat from ★ 2 times **more**; join with slip st to first dc: 16 dc and 8 sps.

Rnd 3: Ch 3, dc in next dc, (2 dc, ch 3, 2 dc) in next ch-3 sp, dc in next 2 dc, ch 2, ★ dc in next 2 dc, (2 dc, ch 3, 2 dc) in next ch-3 sp, dc in next 2 dc, ch 2; repeat from ★ 2 times **more**; join with slip st to first dc: 32 dc and 8 sps.

Rnd 4: Ch 3, dc in next 3 dc, (2 dc, ch 3, 2 dc) in next ch-3 sp, dc in next 4 dc, ch 2, ★ dc in next 4 dc, (2 dc, ch 3, 2 dc) in next ch-3 sp, dc in next 4 dc, ch 2; repeat from ★ 2 times **more**; join with slip st to first dc: 48 dc and 8 sps.

Rnd 5: Ch 3, dc in next 5 dc, (2 dc, ch 3, 2 dc) in next ch-3 sp, dc in next 6 dc, ch 2, ★ dc in next 6 dc, (2 dc, ch 3, 2 dc) in next ch-3 sp, dc in next 6 dc, ch 2; repeat from ★ 2 times **more**; join with slip st to first dc: 64 dc and 8 sps.

Rnd 6: Ch 3, dc in next 7 dc, (2 dc, ch 3, 2 dc) in next ch-3 sp, dc in next 8 dc, ch 2, ★ dc in next 8 dc, (2 dc, ch 3, 2 dc) in next ch-3 sp, dc in next 8 dc, ch 2; repeat from ★ 2 times **more**; join with slip st to first dc, finish off: 80 dc and 8 sps. ✣

#11 ●●○○ Easy

Yarn Requirements for one square:

Color B - 26 yards (24 meters)

Color F - 26 yards (24 meters)

With Color B, ch 25.

Row 1 (Right side)**:** Sc in second ch from hook and in next ch, dc in next 4 chs, (sc in next 4 chs, dc in next 4 chs) twice, sc in last 2 chs changing to Color F in last sc *(Fig. 4a, page 29)*: 24 sts.

Note: Loop a short piece of yarn around any stitch to mark Row 1 as **right** side.

Row 2: Ch 3 **(counts as first dc, now and throughout)**, turn; dc in next sc, sc in next 4 dc, (dc in next 4 sc, sc in next 4 dc) twice, dc in last 2 sc.

Row 3: Ch 3, turn; dc in next dc, sc in next 4 sc, (dc in next 4 dc, sc in next 4 sc) twice, dc in last 2 dc changing to Color B in last dc *(Fig. 4b, page 29)*.

Row 4: Ch 1, turn; sc in first 2 dc, dc in next 4 sc, (sc in next 4 dc, dc in next 4 sc) twice, sc in last 2 dc.

Row 5: Ch 1, turn; sc in first 2 sc, dc in next 4 dc, (sc in next 4 sc, dc in next 4 dc) twice, sc in last 2 sc changing to Color F in last sc.

Rows 6-18: Repeat Rows 2-5, 3 times; then repeat Row 2 once **more**.

Finish off. ✤

#12 ●●○○ Easy+

Yarn Requirements for one square:
Color B - 56 yards (51 meters)

Ch 24.

Row 1 (Right side)**:** Hdc in third ch from hook **(2 skipped chs count as first hdc)** and in each ch across: 23 hdc.

Note: Loop a short piece of yarn around any stitch to mark Row 1 as **right** side.

Row 2: Ch 2 **(counts as first hdc, now and throughout)**, turn; hdc in next hdc and in each hdc across.

To work Front Post treble crochet *(abbreviated FPtr)*, YO twice, insert hook from **front** to **back** around post of st indicated *(Fig. 3, page 29)*, YO and pull up a loop (4 loops on hook), (YO and draw through 2 loops on hook) 3 times.

Row 3: Ch 2, turn; hdc in next 2 hdc, work FPtr around each of next 2 hdc 2 rows **below** (on Row 1), skip next 2 hdc from last hdc made, ★ hdc in next hdc, work FPtr around each of next 2 hdc 2 rows **below** (on Row 1), skip next 2 hdc from last hdc made; repeat from ★ across to last 3 hdc, hdc in last 3 hdc: 11 hdc and 12 FPtr.

Row 4: Ch 2, turn; hdc in next hdc and in each st across: 23 hdc.

To work Front Post double treble crochet *(abbreviated FPdtr)*, YO 3 times, insert hook from **front** to **back** around post of st indicated *(Fig. 3, page 29)*, YO and pull up a loop (5 loops on hook), (YO and draw through 2 loops on hook) 4 times.

Row 5: Ch 2, turn; hdc in next 2 hdc, ★ † skip next 2 FPsts 2 rows **below**, work FPdtr around each of next 2 FPsts 2 rows **below**, skip next 2 hdc from last hdc made, hdc in next hdc, working in **front** of last 2 FPdtr made, work FPdtr around each of 2 skipped FPsts, skip next 2 hdc from last hdc made †, hdc in next hdc; repeat from ★ once **more**, then repeat from † to † once, hdc in last 3 hdc.

Row 6: Ch 2, turn; hdc in next hdc and in each st across: 23 hdc.

Row 7: Ch 2, turn; hdc in next 2 hdc, work FPtr around each of next 2 FPsts 2 rows **below**, skip next 2 hdc from last hdc made, hdc in next hdc, ★ skip next 2 FPsts 2 rows **below**, work FPdtr around each of next 2 FPsts 2 rows **below**, skip next 2 hdc from last hdc made, hdc in next hdc, working **behind** last 2 FPdtr made, work FPdtr around each of 2 skipped FPsts, skip next 2 hdc from last hdc made, hdc in next hdc; repeat from ★ once **more**, work FPtr around each of next 2 FPsts 2 rows **below**, skip next 2 hdc from last hdc made, hdc in last 3 hdc.

Repeat Rows 4-7 for pattern until piece measures approximately 6½" (16.5 cm) from beginning ch, ending by working a **wrong** side row.

Finish off. ✤

General Instructions

Abbreviations

ch(s)	chain(s)
cm	centimeters
dc	double crochet(s)
dc2tog	double crochet 2 together
dtr	double treble crochet(s)
FPdtr	Front Post double treble crochet(s)
FPst(s)	Front Post stitch(es)
FPtr	Front Post treble crochet(s)
mm	millimeters
Rnd(s)	Round(s)
sc	single crochet(s)
sp(s)	space(s)
st(s)	stitch(es)
tr	treble crochet(s)
YO	yarn over

Symbols & Terms

★ — work instructions following ★ as many **more** times as indicated in addition to the first time.

† to † — work all instructions from first † to second † **as many** times as specified.

( ) or [ ] — work enclosed instructions **as many** times as specified by the number immediately following **or** work all enclosed instructions in the stitch or space indicated **or** contains explanatory remarks.

colon (:) — the number given after a colon at the end of a row or round denotes the number of stitches or spaces you should have on that row or round.

Gauge

Exact gauge is **essential** for proper size. Before beginning your project, make a sample square in the yarn and hook specified in the individual instructions. After completing the square, measure it, counting your stitches and rows or rounds carefully. If your square is larger or smaller than specified, **make another, changing hook size to get the correct gauge.** Keep trying until you find the size hook that will give you the specified gauge.

Back or Front Loops Only

Work only in loop(s) indicated by arrow *(Fig. 1)*.

Fig. 1

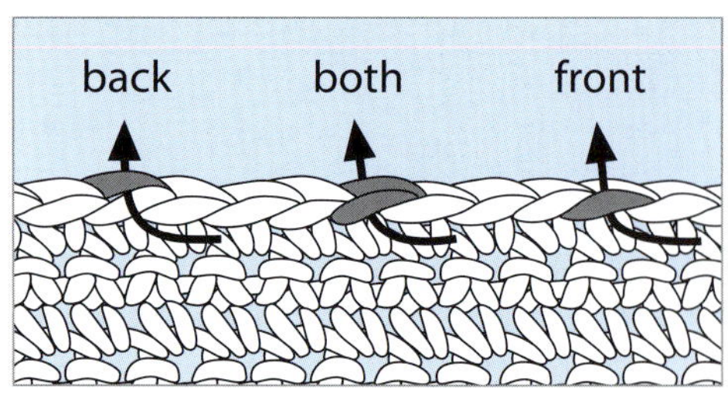

CROCHET TERMINOLOGY		
UNITED STATES		INTERNATIONAL
slip stitch (slip st)	=	single crochet (sc)
single crochet (sc)	=	double crochet (dc)
half double crochet (hdc)	=	half treble crochet (htr)
double crochet (dc)	=	treble crochet (tr)
treble crochet (tr)	=	double treble crochet (dtr)
double treble crochet (dtr)	=	triple treble crochet (ttr)
triple treble crochet (tr tr)	=	quadruple treble crochet (qtr)
skip	=	miss

BEGINNER	Projects for first-time crocheters using basic stitches. Minimal shaping.
EASY	Projects using yarn with basic stitches, repetitive stitch patterns, simple color changes, and simple shaping and finishing.
INTERMEDIATE	Projects using a variety of techniques, such as basic lace patterns or color patterns, mid-level shaping and finishing.
EXPERIENCED	Projects with intricate stitch patterns, techniques and dimension, such as non-repeating patterns, multi-color techniques, fine threads, small hooks, detailed shaping and refined finishing.

Free Loops

After working in Back or Front Loops Only on a row or round, there will be a ridge of unused loops. These are called the free loops. Later, when instructed to work in the free loops of the same row or round, work in these loops *(Fig. 2)*.

Fig. 2

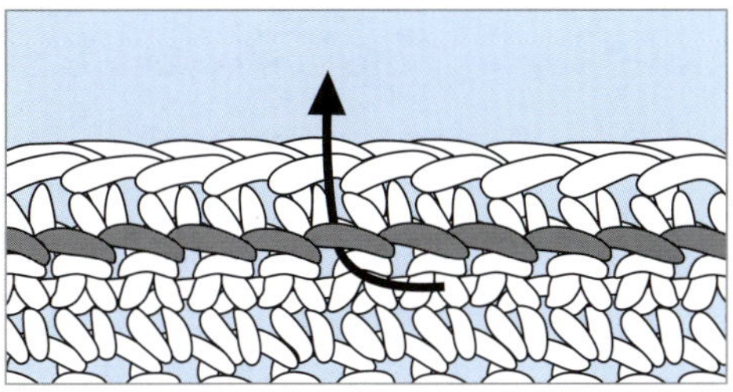

Post Stitch

Work around post of stitch indicated, inserting hook in direction of arrow *(Fig. 3)*.

Fig. 3

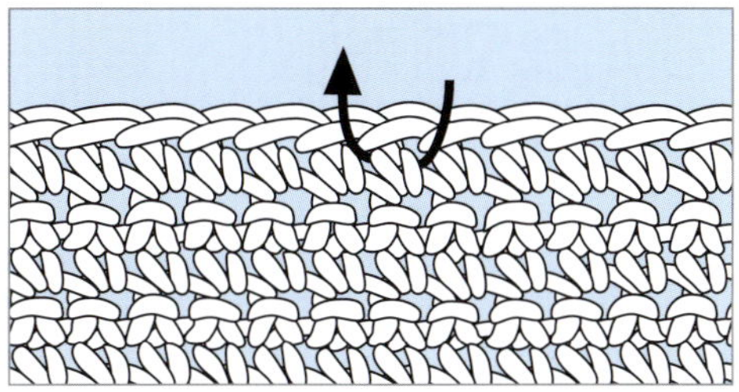

Changing Colors

Work the last stitch to within one step of completion (2 loops on hook), drop yarn to wrong side, hook new yarn *(Figs. 4a & b)* and draw through both loops on hook.

Fig. 4a

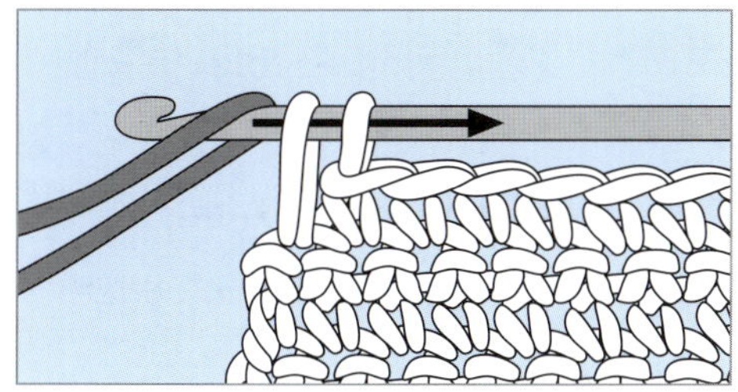

Fig. 4b

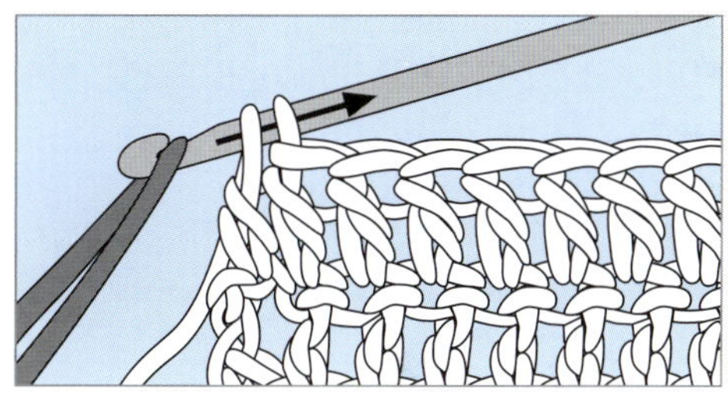

Yarn Weight Symbol & Names	LACE 0	SUPER FINE 1	FINE 2	LIGHT 3	MEDIUM 4	BULKY 5	SUPER BULKY 6	JUMBO 7
Type of Yarns in Category	Fingering, size 10 crochet thread	Sock, Fingering, Baby	Sport, Baby	DK, Light Worsted	Worsted, Afghan, Aran	Chunky, Craft, Rug	Super Bulky, Roving	Jumbo, Roving
Crochet Gauge* Ranges in Single Crochet to 4" (10 cm)	32-42 sts**	21-32 sts	16-20 sts	12-17 sts	11-14 sts	8-11 sts	6-9 sts	5 sts and fewer
Advised Hook Size Range	Steel*** 6 to 8, Regular hook B-1	B-1 to E-4	E-4 to 7	7 to I-9	I-9 to K-10½	K-10½ to M/N-13	M/N-13 to Q	Q and larger

*GUIDELINES ONLY: The chart above reflects the most commonly used gauges and hook sizes for specific yarn categories.

** Lace weight yarns are usually crocheted with larger hooks to create lacy openwork patterns. Accordingly, a gauge range is difficult to determine. Always follow the gauge stated in your pattern.

*** Steel crochet hooks are sized differently from regular hooks–the higher the number, the smaller the hook, which is the reverse of regular hook sizing.

CROCHET HOOKS																	
U.S.	B-1	C-2	D-3	E-4	F-5	G-6	7	H-8	I-9	J-10	K-10½	L-11	M/N-13	N/P-15	P/Q	Q	S
Metric - mm	2.25	2.75	3.25	3.5	3.75	4	4.5	5	5.5	6	6.5	8	9	10	15	16	19

Working in Front of or Around A Stitch

Work in stitch or space indicated, inserting hook in direction of arrow *(Fig. 5)*.

Fig. 5

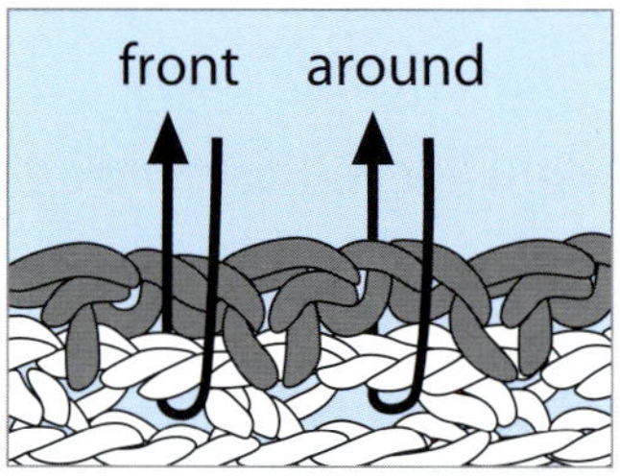

Whipstitch

Place two Squares or strips with **wrong** sides together. Beginning in center of corner, sew through both pieces once to secure the beginning of the seam, leaving an ample yarn end to weave in later. Insert the needle from **front** to **back** through both loops/layer(s) on **both** pieces *(Figs. 6a or b)*. Bring the needle around and insert it from **front** to **back** through next loops/layer(s) on **both** pieces. Continue in this manner across ending in next corner and keeping the sewing yarn fairly loose.

Fig. 6a

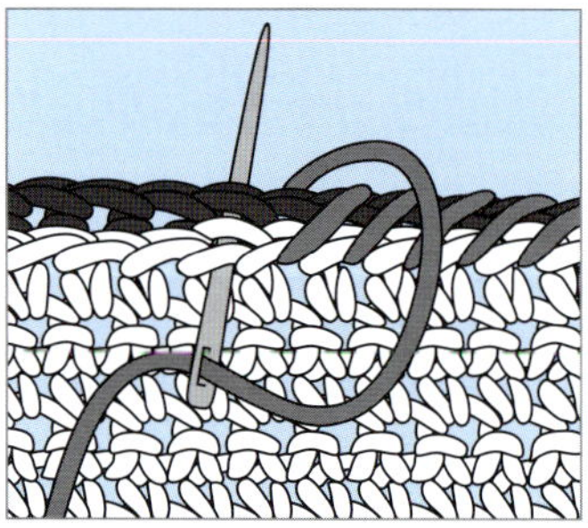

Fig. 6b

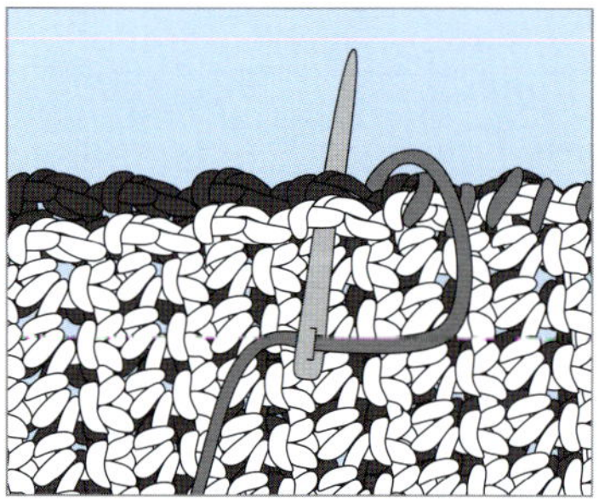

Reverse Single Crochet (abbreviated reverse sc)

Working from **left** to **right**, ★ insert hook in st to right of hook *(Fig. 7a)*, YO and draw through, under and to left of loop on hook (2 loops on hook) *(Fig. 7b)*, YO and draw through both loops on hook *(Fig. 7c)* **(reverse sc made,** *Fig. 7d)*; repeat from ★ around.

Fig. 7a

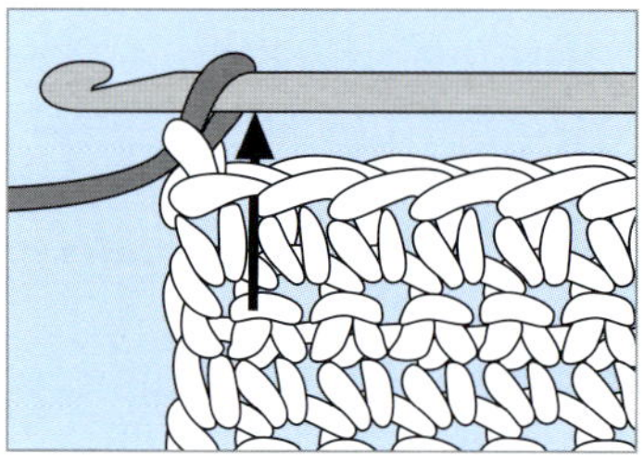

Fig. 7b

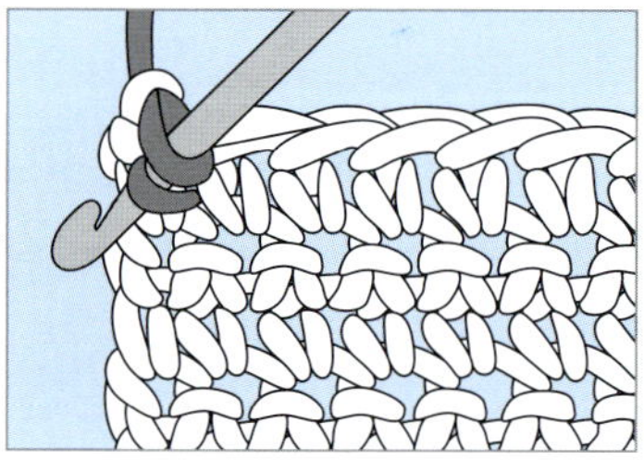

Fig. 7c

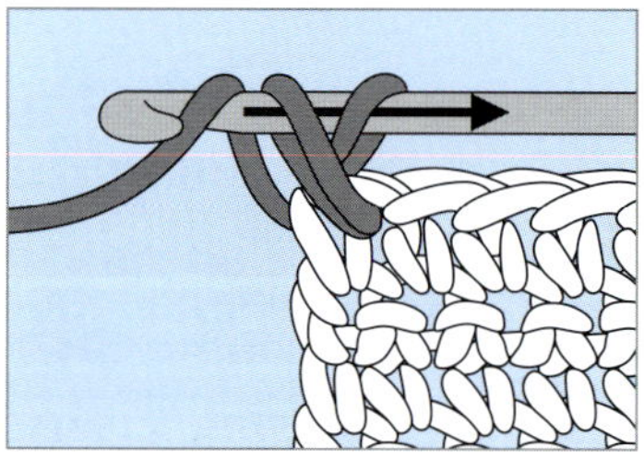

Fig. 7d

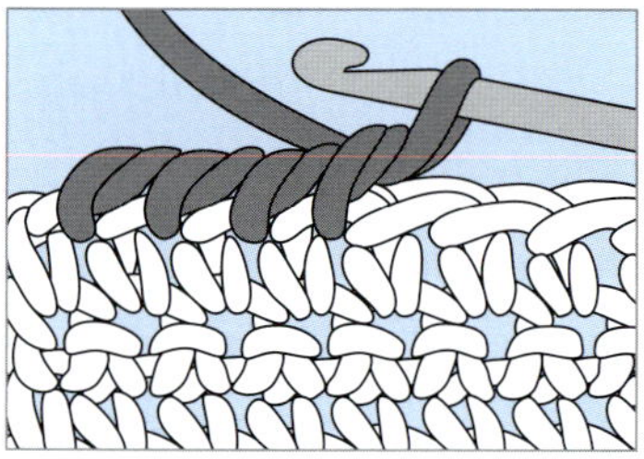

Blocking

Follow the instructions on the yarn label or block as follows:

For wool, steam the Square supporting the weight of the iron at all times. Allow the Square to dry flat, away from heat or sunlight.

For synthetic and blends, submerge the Square in cool water. Roll the Square in a clean terry towel and gently press out the excess moisture. Lay the Square flat and allow to dry completely, away from heat and sunlight.

Yarn Information

The designs in this book were made using ***Red Heart®*** ***Soft Baby Steps®***. Any brand of Medium Weight Yarn may be used. It is best to refer to the yardage/meters when determining how many balls or skeins to purchase. Remember, to arrive at the finished size, it is the GAUGE/ TENSION that is important, not the brand of yarn.

For your convenience, listed below are the colors used to create our photography models. Because yarn manufacturers make frequent changes in their product lines, you may sometimes find it necessary to use a substitute yarn or to search for the discontinued product at alternate suppliers (locally or online).

Sampler

Jade - #9530 Jadie
Blue - #9802 Deep Sky
White - #9600 White
Aqua - #9505 Aqua
Yellow - #9200 Baby Yellow
Bright Green - #9630 Lime
Purple - #9536 Light Grape

Checkerboard

#9802 Deep Sky

Patchwork

Blue - #9802 Deep Sky
Jade - #9530 Jadie
White - #9600 White
Aqua - #9505 Aqua
Purple - #9536 Light Grape

Cuddle-Up Baby

Yellow - #9200 Baby Yellow
Jade - #9530 Jadie
White - #9600 White
Aqua - #9505 Aqua

Naptime

Bright Green - #9630 Lime
Yellow - #9200 Baby Yellow
Jade - #9530 Jadie

Stitch Gallery

Color A (Yellow) - #9200 Baby Yellow
Color B (Jade) - #9530 Jadie
Color C (Bright Green) - #9630 Lime
Color D (Blue) - #9802 Deep Sky
Color E (Purple) - #9536 Light Grape
Color F (White) - #9600 White
Color G (Aqua) - #9505 Aqua

Meet the Designer
Melissa Leapman

With more than 800 knit and crochet designs in print, Melissa Leapman is one of the most widely published American designers working today.

She began her design career by freelancing for leading ready-to-wear design houses in New York City. She also created designs to help top yarn companies promote their new and existing yarns each season. Her ability to quickly develop fully envisioned garments put her skills in great demand.

Through the years, Leisure Arts has published more than 40 books of Melissa's fabulous designs. Melissa is also the host of several Leisure Arts DVDs in the best-selling teach-yourself series, "I Can't Believe I'm Knitting" and "I Can't Believe I'm Crocheting."

Nationally, her designs have been featured in numerous magazines, and her workshops on knitting and crochet are consistently popular with crafters of all skill levels. She has taught at major events such as STITCHES, Vogue Knitting LIVE, and The Knitting Guild Association conferences, as well as at hundreds of yarn shops and local guild events across the country.

To find more of Melissa's designs, visit LeisureArts.com, Facebook, and Ravelry.

We have made every effort to ensure that these instructions are accurate and complete. We cannot, however, be responsible for human error, typographical mistakes, or variations in individual work.

Production Team: Instructional/Technical Editor - Linda A. Daley; Editorial Writer - Susan Frantz Wiles; Senior Graphic Artist - Lora Puls; Photo Stylist - Lori Wenger; and Photographers - Ken West and Jason Masters.

Instructions tested and photo models made by Raymelle Greening, Kimberly Holloway, Nikoma Klein, Amanda Loggins, and Barbara Schou.